When Love Stands Still, Move On!

by

Cheryl E. Williams

AuthorHouse™
1663 Liberty Drive
Bloomington, IN 47403
www.authorhouse.com
Phone: 1-800-839-8640

First published by AuthorHouse 3/22/2011

ISBN: 978-1-4567-3139-7 (sc)
ISBN: 978-1-4567-3141-0 (dj)
ISBN: 978-1-4567-3140-3 (e)

Library of Congress Control Number: 2011901342

Printed in the United States of America

This book is printed on acid-free paper.

Table of Contents

Acknowledgments

"When Loves Stands Still, Move On" is a story inspired by many relationship experiences, including my own. I've taken pieces of a relationship experience that was very special to me for a very long time, and put it together with stories of other women who found themselves in relationships that did not give them the happiness that they wanted or needed.

Writing this book has helped me to see more clearly the things that I have done wrong in relationships. These things, I hope to pass on to other women so that they won't make the mistakes that ultimately brought me to the place where I am in my life today.

I'd like to acknowledge my niece, Alexis, who at the tender age of fifteen, has always given me encouragement in the writing of this book. She's shown as much excitement about this work as she did with my first book. I hope this book will be a guide to her as she gets older and finds herself in the position of picking just the right man for her. I hope that when it's time for her to make that decision she will let God guide her.

I like to also acknowledge my sister Cynthia, Alexis' mom, for supporting me in the writing of this book and with the re-introduction of my first book. She and Alexis have unselfishly given of their time helping me market my first book and supporting me with my new work. For that I thank them. While I was writing this book it was good to know that there were others who cared about something that was special to me.

Lastly, I like to thank "my friend" for his encouragement and support while writing this book, in spite of the contents of the book. I want to thank him for his personal transparency while helping me to make my book a better read. He reminded me constantly that he has his attorney on speed dial. Mostly I'd like to thank him for being big and strong enough to let me say the things I needed to say.

Foreword

First, I want to thank you for picking up this book. The author Cheryl Williams is my sister. I am writing this foreword because I believe that this book is amazing. This book is a bittersweet love story filled with sadness, encouragement, endurance and hope.

When my sister and I were discussing the name of the book she couldn't decide what it should be called. She considered many different names but I believe this title is perfect. *When Love Stands Still Move On!*

In one of my favorite sections of the book, Chapter 7, the author talks about the other side of love. She writes, "She has convinced herself that relationships are not about love; relationships are about survival. It's about who gets the leg up first. It's about making the right decision to do or say the right thing at the right time. Like Gabriela, if you don't make the right decisions, make the right move, say or do the right thing at just the right moment, you will always live in that relationship a few steps behind." I believe that this is so true.

This book is heartfelt and profound. It will put you on an emotional rollercoaster. There will be times when you feel happiness and joy but then everything will change and you'll experience sadness and pain.

I am very proud of my sister and I support her in all that she does. This is her second book, and I believe that she is a very determined person and when she puts her mind to it she can succeed in anything she wants to achieve. I hope that when you read this book you are motivated and inspired.

In the end, you will ask yourself "do I know a Gabriela, or better yet, Am I Gabriela?"

Cynthia T. Williams

Introduction

It's been nearly two decades and Gabriela constantly asks herself; what woman in her right mind would stay in a relationship with the same man for so long and no marriage? She felt as if she was the only woman alive who would actually carry on a near twenty year relationship with herself, while pretending there was a man in her life who loved and cared for her as much as she did for him and who valued what they had together.

The years seem to have gone by so fast because she had reached that age where she's not sure if she would ever be wanted or be special to anyone else. If the opportunity ever presented itself would she know what to do or would she even be interested in doing anything at all. After all, even at the end of the road, even if she were able to call it quits, she knows that this man, that she's loved so long, will always be tucked away in her heart. Would she ever really be able to move on?

The years seem to have gone by so slow because eighteen years of time brought heartache, forgiveness, sadness, on and off times together, complications, happiness, hope, loneliness and tears. There was never any fighting or physical or verbal abuse in their relationship. They were actually very good friends. But for her, the relationship was like taking the longest walk of your life. You have no idea when you are going to get to your destination, but every step tires you out more and more, until you decide to turn around and go back home. She's never been able to turn around and go back home.

Gabriela spent years of her life just living in hope. She'd heard all the experts on relationships who tell you how much time you should give a man and if he doesn't commit the way you want, how you should move on; why buy the cow when the milk is free; and how a man will go as far as a woman will let him, but like many women will tell you, when it comes to relationships, after time, love, hope and sex become intertwined, and then you have a problem.

Gabriela knows that better than anyone now. She will probably always carry a sense of sadness, because of all the time that has passed by that she will never be able to get back. She can't go back to do it over and she would never be able to have the relationship, that she so long hoped for, without his wanting the same.

Sometimes Donovan seemed more complicated than anyone will ever know. Expressing himself wasn't much his thing so understanding where he was coming from was very difficult. Getting him to see where she was coming from was even more difficult. Most times he did what he wanted to do. That was just who he was as a man and there wasn't much chance of getting through to him. He holds in the palm of his hands the thing that Gabriela has hoped for and is missing from all of their years together, and she believes that he knows it.

When he looks at them he sees her and him. She sees them.

*****

About Them

Gabriela and Donovan are opposites, but alike. In many ways they exhibit the same personality and the same thinking, but on the other hand, many times, they've taken different sides and have had different views on many things over the years. They have disagreed and sometimes argued over issues, but always with a mutual respect for one another. Maybe that's one of the reasons why they have been able to deal with one another for so many years. Maybe it's the similarities that have helped them to understand and accept one another for so long.

Gabriela is the youngest of three and Donovan is the second youngest of eight children. They were both raised in the same city, in the state next to the Garden State. They happen to fall under the same zodiac sign, having birthdays within days apart.

She was raised in a household with both parents and had, what she remembers, as a normal and for the most part, happy childhood. As the youngest of the three there was a lot that she learned later in life than her two siblings.

Growing up the youngest is sometimes like that. She grew up from a tomboy, into a young lady with shy mannerisms, but with always a strong personality. Raised back then, she and her family would attend church regularly. Sunday was the Lord's day. Like many young adults, she forgot that for a while, but as an adult she attends church regularly and she's challenged to walk the Christian walk everyday.

As a teen, she attended a private high school close to her home. She received a Bachelor's degree from college so one could say that she was fairly educated.

Her career has led her to a managerial position with a company, which Donovan always laughingly refers to as an easy desk job.

Donovan, who is two years younger than Gabriela, being one of eight children, you can just tell, learned early to make his own way. Like Gabriela, he was also raised in a household with both parents.

Gabriela fondly and lovingly refers to him as a hard-working, blue collar worker, with a very strong work ethic. As long as she has known him, he has never been without work. He is the type of man that a son could look up to. He has always been strong, responsible and stable; not what you would expect from the second youngest of eight.

Donovan attended college as well, and for a couple of years he had a promising athletic future, until the passing of his father. He once told Gabriela that after his father died it just changed things for him. After that, he could no longer focus on his life in college and away from home.

Unlike her, he's not shy. He is very laid back though, quiet when he needs to be, and personable enough to put on the charm when he has to.

The thing that she admires about him the most, is that he does not take …, well you know, from anyone; not even her. That's just who he is.

Opposites, a like, they met when they were in their thirties, and even though Donovan has always viewed, what Gabriela considers being lady-like, as bourgeois, there was something about her that caught his attention, years ago, and there was something about him that she grew to love until this day.

For the both of them, it could be the comfort in knowing that you have someone in your life, no matter the differences, who knows and understands you about as much as anyone could, and loves you still, in spite of yourself.

This is their story.

Their relationship just felt how the beginning always feels. It was just what she needed to put all her past relationships behind her; and that she did. She found herself thirty-something, a single mom, and meeting Mr. Right.

Chapter One

(The First Year)

Gabriela and Donovan met years ago at an event that had been thrown by some friends of hers. The funny thing is, even though it was so many years ago, she remembers being interested initially in Donovan's friend and not Donovan, which she would go on to tell Donovan later on in their relationship. The fact that he was not aware of that gave him no pause to pursue her and try to get to know her better.

She recalls even then that Donovan had a quiet confidence about him and a subtle charm. He was a very polite man. You know how when you meet a man and you just know that he was raised right. That night, that was the man she saw in Donovan. He was very attentive to her for most of the evening. She recalls how at the end of the evening he walked her and a friend outside and saw them both to the car and shut each one's door behind them. She remembers thinking how special that was for him to do. So it didn't take long at all for her interest to grow more and more in Donovan and away from his friend.

She knew that she was becoming pretty impressed by Donovan because just some months before, she had vowed off dating anyone for a long time, because her previous relationship had ended bad enough for her to want to pretend that it had never happened. After getting to know Donovan better, however, she took the chance of going against what it was that she had vowed not to do again.

Gabriela thought that she took her time getting to know Donovan. She wanted to at least appear to take her time with the relationship before jumping into anything too quickly. Looking back it was worth it even though their relationship did not end up the way she had hoped it would.

Initially they spent a lot of time talking to one another on the phone, just as if they were in high school, but that was alright with her because they were getting to know each other better. She remembers wondering why such a nice, eligible man was not in a relationship with anyone when she met him. Maybe he was and he just didn't tell her. She was surprised that most times when she called him on the phone he was actually home. It was just unusual to her or maybe she was just not used to that. Maybe as quiet as he kept it, he was waiting for her call as much as she wanted him to be there when she called.

Everything about them together was going great. Well almost everything. Their first sexual encounter was a little shaky, but that's only because it was with a new guy, in a new place, and she was a little nervous, so things did not go as well as they'd hope. They had taken their time so that everything would go right and look what happened.

Luckily for her, Donovan was as patient as he was kind, and they weathered their first time. They would make up for that as time went by.

Their relationship just felt how the beginning always feels. It was just what she needed to put all her past relationships behind her; and that she did. She found herself thirty-something, a single mom, and meeting Mr. Right.

For Gabriela, their first year together could not have been better. She had not been this happy in a long time. She just felt like she deserved this happiness. She met Donovan at a time when things in her life were not going as well as she had hoped. She was trying to raise a child on her own. She was an educated, part-time worker trying to transition back on her feet. She had been down on herself for a while, so the pick me up and excitement that she got from her new relationship with Donovan was exactly what she needed in her life at that time.

Donovan was a hard and dedicated worker; always have been, even today. He loved the work that he did. Knowing that about him made her feel as though if she wanted to keep this man, she had better step up her game. So with encouragement and support from him that's what she did.

Not only did Donovan have a quiet confidence, but he was a strong man. She always thought of him as a man's man. To Gabriela, he was a man that she would always feel safe with. But she came to see that he was also head-strong and stubborn and he was a man who did exactly what he wanted to do. There was not much she could do to change that.

As the years went by she began to realize that the things that she loved about him the most were also the things that made him so difficult to understand and they would be the very things that caused her the most problems. Gabriela was also head-strong and a little stubborn. It would prove later not to be the ideal recipe for a good and working relationship. He would one day tell her that she was a female version of him.

Even so, they still had things in common. They both had children from previous relationships, who clearly they loved very much. They were good parents, and they enjoyed each other's company. They spent time together constantly. And more importantly, at least to Gabriela, they began introducing each other to the other one's family and friends, which is always a major step in any relationship. There was excitement in the family and friends getting to meet the new person that she had been bragging about all that time. Gabriela knew that if he bragged about her to his friends, half as much as she had bragged about him to hers then she was one step closer to having a loving and lasting relationship with him.

She remembers having a one time conversation with Donovan about getting married and going to look at rings. They even discussed what friends they would choose to be in their wedding parties. They talked about what they would name their daughter if they ever had one. That conversation must have occurred right after some intimate moment or a moment when they both felt happiness because they never had that conversation again.

All the signs were there for this to grow into a relationship that was definitely moving in the right direction and for the first year, it did.

In the good times they had a very loving relationship. For both of them love hit very hard. She felt very lucky to have met him. In the good times he took care of her heart.

Chapter Two

(The Good Times)

In the good times they had a loving relationship. For both Gabriela and Donovan, love hit very hard. She felt very lucky to have met him, so much so that she bragged about him to everybody who was anybody to her. He was too good and this relationship was too good to be true. It seemed as if both of them had not felt this way for a long time. They looked forward to their time together and they spent a lot of it together. Gabriela spent so much time at his apartment that she felt it was time for Donovan to be a part of her son's life as well.

In the beginning her son would noticeably have some difficulty accepting that she was giving some of her time and attention to someone else, because for six years it had always been just the two of them. The beginning was a little stormy but she came to realize that it was a good thing to have Donovan in their lives. He taught her things about raising a young boy that she would not have known and as the years went by her son grew to respect having a strong male figure in his life.

In the good times he took care of her heart. He made she and her son feel as if they were his family. He included her son when he spent time out with his own sons. He had two sons and they would all become friends. Her son was always involved with sports and Donovan would take some time to help him with his game. He even offered to pay for her son to attend basketball camp.

Donovan cooked for them regularly. They would both come to realize that cooking was not Gabriela's thing and Donovan was a good cook. Gabriela just felt good with him then. She felt special then. There was no place she'd rather be than with her son and Donovan.

She remembers when she first started going out with Donovan how nervous she would be. The more she began to like him the more nervous she became. His presence made her nervous. The thought of this new relationship now working out made her nervous.

One of the first times that they dated they were on a day cruise. She remembers feeling pretty nervous then. She was always nervous on dates, first or otherwise. Being nervous did not get in the way of her being happy that day. That was the first time that they ever took a picture together. With her eyes closed she could remember how happy they both were taking the picture, a picture which she will always have. She would keep all the pictures that they'd taken together and with their families as a reminder of a happier time.

The first time that she met one of his closest friends, Donovan had taken her to his friend's home for a cookout. It's funny now that she thinks back. She and Donovan showed up at the cookout in matching color shorts and shirts. It may sound kind of cute and corny now, but their relationship was brand new and they were in love. When you're in love, corny doesn't phase you at all.

That was just another time for her to be happy. She knew that it was big that he had taken her to meet one of his best friends and his family. Donovan is not the kind of man that would introduce any woman to his friends, so she knew that was a plus. As time went by she got the opportunity to meet a number of his friends. Even more important than that, he finally took her to meet his mother and eventually she would meet all of his brothers and sisters. She would never really know how they felt about her, because she never really got the chance to develop any long term relationship or friendship with any of them because things would change between she and Donovan much sooner than she ever expected. Maybe his family did not like her and that affected how much further he allowed their relationship to go. Maybe his friends did not like her. She would never really know.

She remembers being invited by him to a party with his friends from work. She remembers it vividly because he bought her a beautiful, expensive black dress that she would never forget. It fit her just right, as if it were made just for her. She had never had anyone purchase anything for her that expensive before. That night was special to her. Meeting his friends from work that night made her feel as if she had become someone special to him.

She'd always wondered what he told his family and friends when he no longer brought her around. They had to wonder and ask because all family and friends want to know what happened when you stop bringing the once significant other around.

The beginning of a relationship is always a good time in anyone's life and that was a good time for Gabriela and even for Donovan. No matter what happens she will always have the memory of good times.

She could tell that something had changed for him. It was as if he did not want their relationship to work any longer and in his mind, like with a lot of men, he wanted out, so he started turning the wheels to make it happen.

Chapter Three

(Something Changed)

The sad thing about Gabriela staying in this relationship for so long, is that what ever occurred to make the relationship change and move in another direction, had occurred early on; after the first year. In retrospect, she can recall some of the changes that occurred, but a year was all it took for her to find herself tied to a man and a friendship that defined who she was as a person. She'd always wondered, at what point did Donovan know, that it would not be easy for her to walk away.

She could tell that something had changed for him. It was almost as if he did not want their relationship to work any longer and in his mind, like with a lot of men, he wanted out, so he started turning the wheels to make it happen. You know how some men use that trick of starting an argument when they want to break up with their woman temporarily or when they just want to be left alone, well it was almost something like that; except there was no turning back.

There was no turning back, because as much as Gabriela loved Donovan, at times they were like two deer locking horns and their horns began to lock, more often then not. The more difficult he made it for her, the stronger she felt she had to be. It was the only way she could remain there; there being in love with this man, and survive at the same time. But all that did was to give him ammunition to use against her whenever he wanted to make her feel like it was because of her things were not working out. It was she who had become controlling and it was she who had become a nag. Gabriela knew that it was more than that, but there would be no way that she would ever get the truth out of him.

It was at that point that the life that they'd spent living so close together the previous year had starting becoming separate. It seemed as if it were part of some plan he had to destroy the relationship that they once had.

Gradually Donovan's life became his life and Gabriela's life became hers. It wasn't the way that she wanted it, but it was the way he wanted it. They would always be in and out of each other's life from that point on. No matter what direction each of their lives had gone in, the road would always lead back to one another, but the relationship would never be what it once was.

When the relationship began to unravel right before her eyes it was initially very difficult to deal with because Gabriela always fitted into the mold of an emotional woman. She took relationships very seriously and she had been hurt before by relationships in the past. She dreaded the thought of having to go through that kind of hurtful experience again, but she knew what the hurt looked liked when she saw it and she knew this was it, again. All she could think of, is how could she let this happen to her again?

It has been so many years that she can't really remember the reason that Donovan used for distancing himself from her the very first time. She felt that he had played this game with her for a year; getting her to play into this "heaven sent" relationship, only to one day change the game on her. She can remember how good he treated her and the nice things he did for her while he was pursuing her. But now the game had changed.

She remembers seeing him out somewhere where she frequented with friends. He was sitting at the bar, watching a basketball game at the time with mutual friends. At the time their friends may or may not have known that they were no longer together.

It happened to be Valentine's Day, and Gabriela remembers him pulling her close to him by her waist, and whispering to her; "aren't you going to give me a kiss for Valentine's Day?"; and she did.

Gabriela really loved him and missed him by this time and never knowing what was going on in his head, she thought it was a good thing that they'd kissed. Not only did they kiss, but they made plans to see each other later on that night. They got together at his place and they made love as they had always done. It seemed like nothing had changed. At first, she was kind of excited. After all, it was Valentine's Day, and they just happened to see each other and now they even arranged to spend time together. But of course, after making love, she realized that this night would not be theirs together, because he had plans to be somewhere else. She guessed when he ran into her and they kissed, that Donovan saw an opportunity; Gabriela saw a chance.

That night may have been the turning point of their whole relationship. That night may have been the moment that Donovan realized that he could do whatever he wanted and still have Gabriela around. It was then that Gabriela allowed Donovan to "have his cake, and eat it too". At the time it seemed like it was o.k. for Gabriela to get together with Donovan. After all, she wanted to make love to him just as much as he wanted it, but it was then that she allowed the once special relationship between she and Donovan to become nothing more than a relationship on call.

After that, they began to have an on an off relationship. They always kept in contact with one another. They would be together for awhile and then for some reason or another they were not together. They always had an intimate relationship, whether they had not seen each other in months or in years.

And as if their relationship had not been destroyed enough, Gabriela would unintentionally hurt him in a way that he would come to forgive but he would never be able to forget. She knew how badly she had hurt him, but she could not take the hurt back and she could not change what happened. Maybe he would never see her quite the same again, but however on and off the relationship was between the two of them, they kept it going.

In the meantime all of this was very hurtful and still confusing for Gabriela. It was hard because it was happening, but it was harder because who could she talk to about it. She was too embarrassed to tell her friends, because they were the very friends that she had bragged about him to the year before. So she just went on pretending like things had been the same as they once were.

Donovan would later tell Gabriela that he was leaving her to be with someone else. She respected the fact that Donovan was man enough to come and let her know what his intentions were, but it didn't change how hurt she was by the news. She was not prepared for it at all. Even with their ups and downs she never expected him to come and tell her that he wanted to be with someone else.

Earlier that day Donovan had gone to the first Million Man March in Washington, D.C. Gabriela had become a casualty of that experience. That evening he told her about his experience at the March that day. Unfortunately for her the March would change the course of their life. Maybe the March just reinforced feelings that he had been carrying for a while; feelings of being there with those he considered his family; his children and their mother.

Gabriela sat and just looked at Donovan while he talked. She did not know what to say. But she knew him, and she knew that his mind was made up and that there was nothing she could say or do to change it. Out of all the times that she felt she needed to maintain some control, this was it. She did not express any confusion, she did not beg for any whys from him and she could not show any tears, because she knew it would not change what he had already made up his mind to do. She also knew that this was not a spur of the moment decision for him. He had been carrying these feelings for a while. The March just helped him to decide which life he would choose and with whom. All that was left for him to do was to get up enough nerve to tell her about it.

Oddly enough, and not at his request, but because it was what she wanted to do, she made love to him for what she thought would be the last time; and then he left.

She remembers him coming to see her. It was then that he told her what he had done.

Chapter Four

(The Marriage)

When Donovan first left, after a while, Gabriela attempted to rekindle a relationship with an old boyfriend that she had loved in her past. That relationship was short lived. She realized that he wouldn't be able to offer her any more than he did in their past.

Some time had gone by and Gabriela had not been able to successfully have a relationship with anyone else. She made a few attempts at dating, or a few attempts were made on her, but nothing really came of those dates. As a matter of fact throughout all those years Gabriela was never able to establish a relationship with anyone else. She had always loved Donovan and for reasons of her own, she just couldn't see herself being with anyone else. The way in which Donovan left just did not allow her to have closure with their relationship, even though he had moved on for good; or so she thought.

It was not much later, after he left that Gabriela found out that he had eventually married the woman he left her for. She remembers him coming to see her. It was then that he told her what he had done. She'd always felt the need to be in control of herself, so she could not show how much it hurt when he shared the news with her that he had gotten married. She loved him and she really felt helpless. She didn't understand what he was trying to do to her. Even so she didn't think that it was an easy thing for him to tell her and she knew that he cared enough about her still, to come and face her when he did.

Gabriela did not expect that news from him, just as she did not expect the news before. What was strange, though, is that before he came to see her, she felt as if something was wrong. She thought it strange that he had not contacted her in a while, because he always did, and when he came to her job and told her about the marriage, she understood why he had not been able to talk to her before now.

How could this have happened, she thought; how could he marry someone, and it not be her? It was bad enough that she had to deal with the news that he was leaving, but now she had to deal with the news of his marriage. After all he had always claimed to love her.

Gabriela had been down on herself enough, because the man she loved had left her. No one could imagine how she felt when she found out that he married someone else. As a woman, this would just haunt her for years to come. How could this man claim that he loved her, yet marry someone else? She just could not understand it and more than that she knew that it would stay in her mind forever. She would never be able to shake herself from that question, and because through the years she would continue to see him, never having been asked by him to marry, it would never leave her.

Just as in the past, when they broke up, she thought the relationship was over. When she heard the news of his marriage she knew it was over; but it didn't end there.

Time had passed by and she heard from him again. From that point on, the on again, off again relationship, was on again. It really was not the intention of either of them to start up a relationship again, but it happened, as if nothing had changed between them. Something had change though; he was married now. She really didn't know what place he was in his life or in his marriage that he would contact her, but as she had always been before, she was happy to hear from him.

At first, Gabriela and Donovan did not take being together lightly, because he was married, but as time went on it seemed like it became easier and easier to put it out of their minds, at least during the times that they were together.

She could not believe that she allowed herself to be in that place with any man. She had always taken pride in the fact that she had never and would never be with a married man, but she had convinced herself that this was different because this was Donovan and she loved him. She never told him that she was angry that he would claim to love her and allow her to be brought into such a mess. She knew that even though he had walked away and gotten married, that in the back of his mind or his heart he didn't want her to have a relationship with anyone else. He wanted her to be there for him. He would always make sure of that.

Gabriela had the strength for most things, but she just didn't have the strength to not be with him, and even though she really loved him, she would always be ashamed of what she had done. She would always feel terrible about carrying on a relationship with a married man. Even with the guilt, they spent every time that he could spare, together.

Again she had let Donovan know that she would stand for less than she deserved.

She'd always loved him. Where else would she go? Who else could she ever love? She'd convinced herself that Donovan would be the last man that she'd ever love; the last man that she'd ever want to love.

Chapter Five

(Maybe Now)

Gabriela was not surprised at all when she found out that Donovan was no longer with his wife. He had not gotten a divorce, but for whatever the reasons, his marriage had ended, or so he said. He never spoke much about his marriage but he did tell Gabriela that it was over. She never felt that she was the reason for the marriage ending, but she did feel that her being in Donovan's life must have given him less reason to try to make his marriage work. She wasn't even sure if the marriage had ended completely like he said, or was it still going on. She just didn't know. She just took everything in stride. She listened to what little information she could get from him, and went on with the relationship as usual, even though there was nothing usual about their relationship.

Gabriela wondered whether Donovan ever really wanted to get married or did he marry for the wrong reasons. It was easier for her to accept the reality that he married someone other then her, whom she thought and whom he said he loved, if she could convince herself that he had married for the wrong reasons; not because he loved the other woman.

Now that the marriage had ended what did this mean for the two of them. Gabriela had tried to put the marriage behind her because she would never be able to forget it. She thought maybe now Donovan realized that it was her that he loved and maybe now would be their time, but Gabriela soon found out that nothing would change. The only thing that changed, as far as she knew, was that he was no longer with his wife.

Gabriela was in her thirties when they met and now she was in her forties. She didn't know where the time had gone, but she knew that she was still in this relationship. She thought about how foolish she must have appeared to him; this man who left her for another woman, then married the other woman, leaving Gabriela heartbroken, and then she allowed him to come back into her life while he was married and she continued to carry on with the relationship even after the marriage. It was too embarrassing to even tell her friends.

He could see that Gabriela had expected and hoped that now that he was no longer with his wife he would be ready to commit himself to her. But it was not what he wanted. So now he had to find ways to continue to see her, just because he could; still without any commitment.

She doesn't put all the blame in this relationship on Donovan, because she understood the decision to continue seeing him was hers. She felt that she had already spent so much time in this relationship, why should she let go now. After all, she had become so comfortable with him that the thought of being with someone else just didn't work for her. Even though she considered it many times, the thought of being with anyone else while being with him at the same time, was not an easy thing for her to do. Even though she loved him, she really wanted to move on, but she just didn't know how and he would never make it easy for her to do.

In her heart she always felt that Donovan made the decision long ago that he would never marry her, and for not being straightforward and honest about that, she does blame him. He had become content with just having an intimate relationship with her at his leisure, because she let him.

He always knew how difficult it was for her to leave him. He became aware of that a long time ago. He always tested her in different ways because he knew it. He had learned just the things to say to her, and just the things to do with her so that she would stay around. The problem was that the things he said never matched up with what was going on in their relationship.

Gabriela started to realize how unhappy their relationship was making her. She was always happy for the times that they were able to spend together, but every time he left, she was always unhappy with herself, because she knew that continuing to see him was not the right thing for her. She was unhappy with the relationship they had together and she was unhappy when he was not around.

Donovan always had a nonchalant attitude about their relationship, so she constantly questioned whether he loved her or not. He would always ask her why is it that she felt he didn't love her as if he thought that his love for her was obvious. It was as if the two of them were in two different relationships. His love for her was never obvious to her.

In the years following, things would remain the same. He became very content with carrying on the relationship as they always did.

Gabriela tried so hard to express how she felt about the lack of commitment in their relationship. She always found it difficult to understand Donovan. Their relationship was very complicated and maybe that was by design; she just never knew.

Donovan always seemed to have a side to him that was hard to reach. When he felt he wanted to talk to her that is when she heard from him. When he was in a good mood, that's when he would bring some happiness to their time together. There were times when he made her feel like he wanted to spend time with her and then there were days when he was there, but not so much there.

There were times when she did not hear from him or talk to him for days at a time. When she called him on the phone she could tell by the sound of his hello, which was "hey", whether she should take the conversation much further.

Through the years she didn't understand him and there were times when she would not handle his personality in a way that would be beneficial to her. But being in a relationship with Donovan over time, and maturing herself, she would learn to deal better with the man that he was.

She'd always loved him. Where else would she go? Who else could she ever love? She'd convinced herself that Donovan would be the last man that she'd ever love; the last man that she'd ever want to love.

Gabriela knew that she had made a major relationship blunder; letting him think that anything goes, because anything did and would

Chapter Six

(The Last Man She'd Ever Love)

After the marriage ended Gabriela felt as though her relationship with Donovan had not gotten any better. She was still being treated like the other woman and that would continue throughout their relationship. She hadn't noticed it at first, but as time went on she realized that she and Donovan would never do anything together, outside of the house. They never went anywhere or did anything as a couple. He didn't take her around his family or his friends as he once did. It was as if, to anyone else, she did not exist.

Whenever she discussed this with Donovan, which was frequently, he would always have an excuse for why he was not able to do the things she wanted to do; the normal things that couples do all the time.

His reason was that he worked to hard; to hard to do regular things like going out to dinner. He would tell her that he knows that she expects a lot of his time, but that because of his schedule he was unable to give her the time and the commitment that she needed. Unfortunately for her, one time turned into many times over the years, times they would not spend outside of her home.

Quite naturally, Gabriela wondered, what was going on with Donovan? Were there other women? Was he still married? Did he get back with his wife and hadn't figured out how to tell her yet? Or did he realize that Gabriela would continue to see him no matter what he did? If he were not seeing another woman, it always seemed as if he were.

Gabriela knew that she had made a major relationship blunder; letting him think that anything goes, because anything did and would.

Gabriela felt as if Donovan had started to take advantage of their situation, and of her; at least that's how it appeared to her. He knew that he would not have to do anything differently. He knew that he would not have to change anything.

Gabriela knew that if she really wanted to confirm a relationship with any other woman, there were ways to do it and she thought about it many times; just to prove that he was being sneaky and dishonest, but to take that route was just not her style.

That was something else that Donovan knew about her, that's why everything always worked to his advantage when she accused him of being with other women. He knew that all he had to do was to deny, deny, deny. So she had two options; she could change who she was and go find out what she needed to know or she could just trust him. Well there was one other option; she could leave him, but she wouldn't.

Every single day, it became more difficult for her to accept the relationship the way it was and to trust the things that Donovan would tell her. She'd always felt emotionally trapped. She'd always loved him. Where else would she go? Who else could she ever love? She'd convinced herself that Donovan would be the last man that she'd ever love; the last man that she'd ever want to love.

Feeling emotionally trapped motivated her to try to leave the relationship and him more than once. She would always get to that point where she could just not take what was going on any longer. She'd get to that point where she could no longer take him not understanding how she'd felt, or understanding it but not be willing to change things.

So there were a number of times where Gabriela would just tell Donovan that it was over. She'd always felt that she was giving him the opportunity to leave and live the life that he wanted to live without holding on to her. She knew that his leaving was better for her. She could condition herself to be alone as long as she knew she had no man in her life, but it was so much harder dealing with being alone when he was there, but not really.

They would break up on a number of occasions and they would not see each other or talk to each other for months. Each time they would break up, as much as she missed having him in her life, she found it easier to be without him. She always knew that she was doing the right thing for her.

The closer that she would come to getting over the hump of being without Donovan, she would always hear from him. It was as if he knew that he needed to contact her in the "nick of time" not to allow her to be able to make it without him for good. Maybe that was what he was thinking and maybe not. She just didn't know for sure, but it would always play itself out the exact same way.

Whatever Donovan's thinking, it would always work for him. She would not have ever called him, but she had been alone so long, that when he did call, she was glad to hear from him, even though letting him back into her life was not the right thing for her to do.

Not only would she allow him back into her life, but she would let him back in, bringing nothing new to the table. He would come back, nothing would change, and she'd be right back where they ended.

They were more than just lovers and friends; they were in what she thought, was a loving relationship; just the kind of relationship that she wanted and with the person she wanted to be with.

Chapter Seven

(The Other Side of Love)

If Gabriela had not learned anything about relationships, she learned this one thing; that love has another side. She came to learn the hard way, that with all the commitment and heart that you put into a relationship, that the other side of love always surfaces, eventually.

Gabriela always finds herself unprepared for what the other side has in store for her, even though she's been through it many times before. As often as she has been in a relationship, she always fell in love with love, or the fun of the relationship. Wonderful, happy times, take over for a few months and then the reality of the "other side", kicks in. Well, thank God for the wonderful, happy times, because once the latter kicks in, she begins to get weighed down with issues ranging from misunderstanding, lack of communication, relationship hopping, imagined or fact, and lots of heartache. The funny thing is that when it all comes down on her, she's always taken off guard, as if it were a surprise.

She's convinced herself that relationships are not about love; relationships are about survival. It's about who gets the leg up first. It's about making the right decision to do or say the right thing at the right time. Like Gabriela, if you don't make the right decisions, make the right move, say the right thing at just the right moment, you will always live in that relationship a few steps behind.

Gabriela could never understand why choosing to love someone has to always become a game; a game of who does what to whom first; a game of who should reveal their love first; a game of when to say yes and when to say no, and a game of what you should and should not allow.

She just never understood why people choose to turn relationships into a game, rather than just be happy. Love and relationships can be so much fun, if people would just let them run their course. The game is always exhausting; yet people choose to play it. And in the game someone always gets hurt.

In this relationship and in others, Gabriela knows that she did not get the "leg up" first. As a matter of fact, she lost her footing a long time ago. She has never been about the game and she would never be good at playing it.

Her relationship with Donovan has been exhausting. She has always been a few steps behind, because as tired as she has become from their relationship, Donovan seemed to be fine with it.

Gabriela has just been disillusioning herself with the hope that one day things will be the same between them; the way they once were. Even though now, they are lovers and friends, she wishes for the day when he treated her as if she were special again.

Donovan did make her feel special, once. They were more than just lovers and friends; they were in what she thought was a loving relationship. They were in the kind of relationship that she wanted, and he was the person she wanted to be with. They spent a lot of time together and they did things together. They enjoyed each other's company.

As it turned out she never really knew what Donovan thought about their relationship. By this time she felt that the times they spent together were just enough time for Donovan to get her where he wanted her.

As much as Gabriela still loves him; as much as she sees him as a friend that she feels close to, she is disappointed in the way that he has left her open to no longer feeling special and important to him. She is disappointed that no matter what she says to him, or how hard she tries to get him to see it, he does not see how her heart has been broken over the years because of them. If this man, she can't even say her man; if this man whom she has known and loved for years, no longer sees her as special, then what man would?

Donovan had expressed his love for Gabriela throughout the years, but what he said just doesn't mean a whole lot, because his actions never seem to match his words.

He'd always tell her that he did not understand why she did not believe that he loved her. It was like they were both living two separate lives, together.

Donovan didn't seem to really want much from the relationship anymore. Intimate times together, some laughs and brief conversations with Gabriela seemed to be all he was willing to bring to the relationship.

When things didn't seem to be going well, he pretended not to notice and he hoped that she would not bring it up. He had become so use to Gabriela expressing her unhappiness about the same things over and over again, that sometimes it just appeared as if he'd listen to her dissatisfaction with the relationship, wait for her to get over it, and he'd then carry on as if nothing was ever said and as if very little needed to change, especially if he had to make any changes.

Donovan had become so use to Gabriela complaining and leaving so many times that it would turn into a game where he'd just wait her out, as if he knew that in the end she would always be there.

Gabriela still hopes for the day, that she will leave him for good, even though she loves him. The thought of leaving for good is also a little scary, because even in his confidence, Gabriela knows that he will never understand what he lost, until the day that she really is gone for good; not just because of the fact that with them there is a feeling of being comfortable with one another, but also because a special friendship will be lost.

There is definite truth to the fact that a person never realizes what they have in another person until that person is gone.

Gabriela always gets the sense that Donovan feels that she should be lucky to have him. Sometimes he tells her that he is a pretty good catch, and there could be some truth to that, but it doesn't really matter if he won't allow himself to be caught.

Maybe Gabriela was too strong for any man to think that she needed him to take care of her and to protect her. She has always had to be strong; at least she felt she had to be. She was a single mother raising a son; showing weakness was not an option for her.

Chapter Eight

(The Comfort of a Man)

Gabriela has never felt like she's ever had a man who really cared about her enough to keep her heart intact. She'd never expected anyone to take care of her financially. She just wanted someone there to support her and to comfort her. She wanted someone she could talk to when she needed to. It would've been nice to have a man to help her to carry burdens that were just too heavy to carry alone. After all, aren't women raised to believe that men are suppose to be around to protect them; to take care of them, and to give them a shoulder to cry on. What happened to those men?

She's never experienced that type of man, not for long. The good times that she had with Donovan didn't last long so she can't really say if she would have had that type of relationship with him. If you asked him he'd probably say that he's always been that to her, but he hasn't; not always.

Maybe she did always pick the wrong man, or maybe she was just too strong for any man to think that she needed him to take care of her and to protect her. She has always had to be strong, or at least she felt she had to be. She was a single mother raising a son, and showing weakness was not an option for her. Things were very hard at times and had she not stayed strong, she would not have gotten through them.

She had to do everything for her son without the help of a man. She was the mother and father at all his sporting events for years. She made sure that he was well educated. Anywhere he had to be, she was responsible for getting him there. She needed to do the little things like sit in barbershops every other weekend, listening to barbershop talk and wondering to herself, why was she there. Shouldn't that be the job of his father? She worked hard, and most of her money went to raising her son. There were many times when she had to borrow money just to pay for bills. That, she never felt good about having to do.

Strangely enough when all this was going on, Donovan was in her life, but she never felt good about asking for his help, so he never knew that she needed the help. Asking for his help would make her appear to be needy and not strong. She had a difficult time showing that side of herself to any man.

That was not the woman she wanted to be; it was the woman she had to be. So maybe a man could not see what it was that she needed.

She remembers many conversations with men, including Donovan, about 21st century women. He would say that 21st century women act as if they don't need a man.

She did not understand why men could not see that no woman wants to do everything on her own; no woman wants to be on her own to prove something to a man.

Gabriela did things on her own for a very long time. She worked hard, raised her son, and took care of any other problems that came along. She did it on her own because she had no other choice. After taking responsibility of everything for so long it becomes very difficult for a woman to step back and relinquish even a little control when a man comes into her life.

Maybe Donovan felt that way about her when they first met. He would never have understood how things were for her when they met. The funny thing is that when they first met she was at her lowest time, and having him come into her life was a Godsend, or at least that's what she had hoped. But even at her lowest time, maybe she was not able to relinquish control. After all, who was this man? She could not relinquish control of herself until he had shown her that it would be safe to do so.

When Gabriela and Donovan met, her son was about six years old. Having him come into her life was good for both she and her son at the time. He taught her things that would help her to raise her son; things that she would not have known on her own. Her son's relationship with Donovan didn't start out so well at first, but that was expected because for a long time it had just been the two of them. Eventually, though her son did grow to like and respect Donovan; then one day he was gone, or at least no longer committed to the relationship.

His leaving made her realize that she could not just bring men in and out of her son's life. That would begin a life of her being alone. She dedicated her life to raising her son. His life became her life.

What started out as a life of being alone turned into a life on and off with Donovan. For a number of reasons, being with him just seemed like the most comfortable thing to do at the time. She had no way of knowing that forever would follow this relationship.

It was hard for her having a man in her life, yet still feeling alone. It affected her the most when she attended any event without the escort of a man; not any man, but the man that she knew she had. She always hated going to functions year after year without him. While he was taking no part in her outside life, she was carrying on her life as if she were involved with no one. It was embarrassing for her to think that people must have wondered for years, why she was always without a man.

Donovan always told her that she worried too much about what other people thought and said, but this had become much bigger than that for Gabriela. It was no longer about what people must have thought; it was about what she thought and how she felt. If people did think that, they were right.

She just wanted to feel special again. Maybe if he could have given a rose from time to time, or bought her a gift or took her out for no particular reason, she would have felt a little special.

Donovan had come to think so little of her, at least that's how she felt, that he'd stopped doing those things. It was so simple. She was not really hard to please and she didn't understand why he did not see that.

These were just little things that would've made her happy; things that he stopped doing. She'd felt that if she was no longer special to him, when he left, he should've stayed gone.

Gabriela knew that walking would give them the opportunity to talk. He didn't talk much but how could he avoid it now. He'd made himself vulnerable to whatever conversation she wanted to have.

Chapter Nine

(The Illusion)

Gabriela and Donovan were taking a vacation together. She was so excited because this was something that she always wanted; for them to be able to go away and take a vacation together. That day was finally here.

They boarded the plane to Cancun and you could see that they were both happy to get away together; away from their jobs and their families, just so they could be by themselves for a change.

She was so excited because with both their salaries they were able to rent a house by the water and this was the first time where she had taken a trip to an island and did not stay in a hotel. This was the first time that she was getting away with just Donovan.

When they arrived in Cancun everything was just beautiful. The weather was perfect, the air smelled great and they were happy. Once they got set up in the beautiful place where they were staying, they walked around for awhile, hand in hand, looking for some place where they would both like to eat. They eventually found a restaurant that was satisfactory to both of them and they had a wonderful dinner.

After dinner they decided to take a walk on the beach. This was especially exciting to Gabriela, because she knew that would give them the opportunity to talk, and she never really got a lot of time to talk with Donovan. He didn't like to talk much but how could he avoid it now. He'd made himself vulnerable to whatever conversation she wanted to have. He'd allowed himself to be alone on an island, on a beach with just her, and no one who meant anything could disturb them. So he just went with the moment.

They made love that evening and everything was perfect. The whole vacation could not have started any better.

Everyday for the next week was filled with a lot of fun. If Donovan had grown tired from being alone with Gabriela all week, it did not show. They took a tour around the island, took a scooter ride throughout the area, spent a day on a boat just relaxing and enjoying the day, and, probably much to Donovan's distaste, they actually spent time shopping. Gabriela convinced him that of course they would need to get souvenirs for their families.

Everyday they would use some time to sit out on the porch overlooking the beach and just talk and enjoy each other's company. After all, Donovan worked so hard, how often would they get a chance to take a trip like this one, so Gabriela was definitely going to make the most of it.

On their last night in Cancun Gabriela began to feel sad because by tomorrow evening their trip would've ended and they would be back to their life at home.

The next day they boarded the plane and Gabriela just sat looking out the window preparing for the plane to takeoff.

Later she thought to herself how wonderful this trip would have been had it actually happened, but it never did. It was just an illusion in her mind. It is the kind of vacation that she'd hoped to have with him for years. It just never happened.

The truth is, that in almost two decades, Gabriela and Donovan have never taken a trip together outside of the state that they lived in. Once she recalls spending a weekend together. She had taken trips without Donovan many times, and Donovan may have taken trips without her; she didn't know.

One thing she always did that Donovan didn't. She would always listen to him when he talked. So many times he made mention of something that would strike a bad chord with her. She remembers having a conversation with him; can't really remember what led to the conversation, but while they were talking Donovan said that he had been on a cruise. He seemed clueless to the fact that she was so upset when he said this. She just sat there and continued to listen to him talk, not challenging what he said. While he continued his conversation she just looked at him, thinking what nerve he had to tell her that he had been on a cruise before. She had known him for many years so he had to go on the cruise somewhere during that time. She never got the impression from him that he would ever be interested in going on a plane anywhere, let alone getting on a ship and cruising on the water. He had never asked her to go away anywhere, but obviously he had no problem with traveling.

Gabriela was so hurt and angry that she could not help but to wonder what other things she didn't know about Donovan. It was those types of things that always made her feel as if she was living her life and he was living his, separately.

Although Donovan tried really hard to make her feel as if she was just a complaining woman, worried about what others said, even he couldn't be so clueless to think that it was normal for them to carry on whatever type of relationship they had and never do things together the way that normal couples do.

Gabriela just wanted to go anywhere together, for a night, a weekend or even longer. What was so hard about that?

She'd always found herself committed to, not bad, but poor relationships with men not worthy of her time or her love, yet she found it difficult to leave.

Chapter Ten

(IN R.E.T.R.O.S.P.E.C.T.)

In retrospect making bad decisions when it came to relationships really didn't start with Donovan. It began many years before him.

Gabriela remembers making bad relationship decisions beginning with her first boyfriend. He was older than she was, a little wiser, street and otherwise. She was seventeen, it would be the first sexual relationship she'd had, and it would be a six year relationship of mistakes.

Firstly, she would give her heart and her body to the wrong man; that had become clear. Even though Gabriela learned a lot from that relationship she would still go on to make future relationship mistakes. She was young, and like many young women, she was not really sure how she should be treated; at least not in the beginning. As the years went by she realized that she deserved better than the man that she'd chosen. She was too young to understand that she had lowered her standards by taking up with him for any length of time; unfortunately for her the relationship lasted too long. He was a man who sensed that he had met a young woman that he could control to a point, so the more she allowed control, the more he took.

It was a relationship that she knew she could no longer be in, but she found it difficult to leave. She'd always found herself committed to, not bad, but poor relationships with men not worthy of her love or her time, yet she found it difficult to leave.

Gabriela knew that it was inevitable that she would one day leave him she just didn't know how or when she would find the strength to do it.

Unfortunately, it took meeting another man for her to finally make her way out of the relationship. Let's face it one way to get over and out of a relationship with the wrong man is to find another man. Soon after, she would realize that taking up with another man was not the answer, but had she not been able to leave him then, she would have allowed him to stay around forever.

Gabriela was relieved when she finally ended their six year relationship. She felt a sense of control herself when she broke off the relationship. She remembers that even though she had lost all interest in him and they were no longer a couple, he would still attempt to be her friend and come around in the hopes that maybe they would get back together. By then she felt really good about herself, because she realized that she had the control back and that he really could not accept that she ended their relationship.

Gabriela had been in a new relationship for a while and by this time she had given birth to a son. Even with the birth of her child, her former boyfriend would come around with offers of marriage and help with raising her child. Of course, typical of Gabriela, by now she was in love with the father of her child, so she had no interest in his "Johnny come lately" offers of help or marriage.

She can't remember what finally made him give up and go away, but by then she really didn't care. She thinks of the relationship from time to time, especially since it was her first. She can't help but think that somehow she has always carried the mistakes that she made in that relationship, with every meaningful relationship to her, to follow. She just can't understand why she always made bad relationship decisions; why she always said yes, when she should have said no; why she pretended to look the other way, when guys treated her less than the way that she knew she deserved to be treated. Sadly, she did not have the answer to those questions then, and she still does not have the answers. She is still asking herself the same questions.

Maybe she just always wanted to feel as if she was needed; she just didn't know. She has been analyzing herself and her mistakes for years. Even if she found the strength to leave Donovan right now, she is afraid that she would make the wrong decisions in meeting someone new, giving her another reason to feel comfortable and safe with Donovan. She really wishes that she could trust Donovan with everything that she is, but deep down inside she knows that she will never really trust Donovan or any other man; not ever again.

They say trust is something you have to earn. Well in the time between her relationship with her first boyfriend and Donovan, a span of thirty years, Gabriela has only been left with the feeling that giving her trust to men, has left her with nothing much to speak of except heartache and wasted years. She wants to believe that her son is not the only good thing that has come out of her relationship misfortunes, but she can't really say what else she's gotten out any of them.

When you're in a relationship with someone as long as she has been with Donovan, you should have something to show for it. You should be able to say that you got something out of it other than just a friendship. After all, she could have had the friendship without anything else and still have the same outcome. She and Donovan would probably have been better off ending their intimate relationship and remaining friends, but that has been a mutual decision that neither of them have been able to commit to.

When Donovan seemed into the relationship, when he seemed as if his heart was really into it, for Gabriela, that was as good as great gets. Just for a little while she'd felt special again.

Chapter Eleven

(As Good As Great Gets)

Gabriela admits that there has been so many times over the years that she'd convinced herself that things were going well with her and Donovan's relationship. There were times when Donovan really turned things up and Gabriela felt maybe their relationship was really worth hanging on to.

Sometimes he just really knew how to turn things on just enough for Gabriela to believe that something new was happening; that something was changing in the relationship. The problem was that when Donovan turned things up like he did, it didn't always last. As quickly and as unexpectedly as he turned things on he would turn things off. Three or four months would go by where he would seem as if he genuinely cared about their relationship; as if he really wanted to be there. He was kind, considerate and funny; and Gabriela really enjoyed seeing that side of him. It was the other side of him that always left her confused, alone and sometimes hurt. It was seeing him go from being engaged in their relationship to quickly becoming disconnected from the relationship. Out of the blue sky, things would just go back as they were before.

Their relationship always left Gabriela with that feeling that you get when things are going well in your life, so well that you just know something is going to come along and ruin things. That's how she felt in her relationship with Donovan.

Maybe to anyone else what Gabriela thought was going well, meant really nothing, but to her, when Donovan seemed involved in the relationship, when he seemed as if his heart was really into it, to

Gabriela that was as good as great got. Just for a little while she'd felt special again.

It was New Year's Eve; another one of many. Gabriela hadn't expected much in the way of spending any time with Donovan, because it had been years since they'd spent New Year's Eve together. It may have only been one time that they spent New Year's Eve together; she wasn't really sure. If it did happen once before, it would have been the year that they first dated. The fact that so many years went by would always bother her, because she always took to heart what she once heard someone say, she doesn't remember who, that how you bring in the New Year is how the New Year would go.

Gabriela couldn't help thinking every year, that it wasn't a good sign for the new year coming that she was not bringing it in with the man that she loved, and every year that she did not bring in the new year with Donovan would be indicative of how the relationship would go that year.

This New Year's Eve was different. Gabriela had just finished up at work and she received a call from Donovan. He asked her was she home, because he wanted to come over. Gabriela said sure and she told him that she would meet him at her house. She didn't expect to spend much time with him, because like always he would have some reason why he had to leave. It was New Year's Eve and she was just happy to be able to spend any amount of time with him.

Donovan arrived at Gabriela's house just a little after she did. When she opened the door and he came in, he came in bearing gifts of food, and before she knew it, Donovan was in the kitchen preparing a New Year's Eve dinner for the both of them.

Even watching him in the kitchen preparing dinner, with no help from her, Gabriela was still a little unhappy when she should've been happy, because she knew that after he was through making dinner, and after they ate and talked for a while, that he would surely leave, and she really did not want him to go. This was the closest that she'd ever come to having him around on New Year's Eve.

As the evening went on she noticed that he had purchased a bottle of champagne and had it chilling in the refrigerator. It was then that she realized that Donovan had planned for them to spend that evening together; at least she'd rather have made that assumption then to dare ask him and get the wrong answer.

He was staying. Donovan had no idea how much that night meant to her. It was a night that she had planned to spend alone, or at least not with him, because they had not spent New Year's Eve together in a long time. What happened that night was just unexpected, but she enjoyed it and it would stay with her for a long time, because that is what she's always wanted to do. She wondered; did he really know how much it meant to her? Whether he knew it or not, he sure got brownie points that night.

It seemed so silly that something that would be so insignificant to another couple, like spending New Year's Eve together, would mean so much to her, but you would have to understand the relationship that she lived to appreciate why it meant so much to her. It was just something that didn't happen, and even if when tomorrow came, things were different, Gabriela was able to share that night with Donovan. For her it was as good as great gets.

She can't help picturing herself standing in a room of strangers feeling invisible and out of place. She knows that's where she belongs, because she has loved him forever, but no one else in the room would know.

Chapter Twelve

(Invisible)

Gabriela felt invisible for so long. So many times she's tried to get Donovan to understand what it is like to feel like she does not exist in his life, outside of just the two of them, but it has never gotten through to him. He just doesn't understand why she has this need for people to know what's going on between them and she doesn't understand why he has a need for people not to know what's going on between them.

She's always had this one concern. What would she do if anything ever happened to Donovan; how would she know; who would know to tell her? She would bring this question up to Donovan again and again over the years. He would brush it off, as if again, he did not understand what this meant to her, by saying that someone would let her know. Again, Gabriela's question would be, who?

Suppose he got sick or even worse; when would she find out. If it happened that she would get sick or even worse, her family and some of her friends would know to contact him and let him know, but if something happened to Donovan, Gabriela feels that she would still be a well kept secret. Donovan had isolated her from the most important people in his life; his family and his friends.

Gabriela can't help picturing herself, standing in a room of strangers, feeling invisible and out of place. She knows that's where she belongs because she has loved him forever, but no one else in the room would know.

Imagine being in a relationship and being in love with someone forever, and they pass away, and you feel out of place; you do not know where your place would be. She can just see herself sitting in a corner alone watching everyone, family and friends, interacting amongst each other, while she sits there grieving to herself, knowing that no one will ever know how much he meant to her and how much she loved him. And if she happened to be acknowledged by someone who remembered her from years ago, she would only be remembered as no more than an old friend of Donovan's coming to pay her respects.

It is just one of those things that Gabriela hopes that she will never have to deal with, and only Donovan can make it so that she never will. She knows that a day will come when they will both go, but for him to leave her like that, would leave her behind in a relationship that will forever be unfinished, and leave her forever invisible.

She's always thought that she and Donovan must have a different idea about what love really should be. For her, when you really love someone, that is not something you want to keep a secret; you wouldn't care who knows about it. When you claim to love someone for nearly two decades, whether it has been in an on and off relationship or not, that should have a special meaning.

It should mean so much to both Gabriela and Donovan, to have someone who has been your friend and has loved you and stuck by you, in spite of everything; all your faults, your moods, and all your life's issues, even without the marriage. That kind of commitment, when you're not even married should not be treated lightly. That kind of relationship should not be invisible.

Gabriela doesn't expect Donovan to go and shout it out to everyone that she's with him and that he's with her. She never needed it to be spoken, she's just always wanted it to be known and understood that she is the special person in his life, and he in hers.

For her, right now, this has been the start of a good year for her and Donovan. He has turned it on again. He is engaged in the relationship, and for right now they are happy, but she's always uncomfortable in knowing that it could change at any time. She hopes it doesn't, because she's happy and when he changes things, she changes, and she's happy with the person that she is now.

Gabriela stepped out on faith one day, and she told Donovan that she would like for them to get married. She thought that they seemed happy enough and after all their time together she didn't feel that it mattered whether she brought up the issue of marriage. What was she thinking? She asked him what he thought of what she said, and his response was that he was not ready to get married. She felt helpless to respond to that. What could she say to a man who has been in a relationship with her for nearly two decades, when he says he's not ready for marriage? It's not as if they were dating for a couple of years, so there was no way that she could come back at him. It's very hard to deal with that kind of hopelessness.

After that conversation, Gabriela had no reason to believe that Donovan would ever want to marry her. She does not even know how much it really matters anymore. She does know this; that it will always stick with her, that he never thought her worthy to ask.

Maybe marriage is just too much for Donovan to handle again; who knows, but for Gabriela being invisible is just as hard.

Like Gabriela, most women know what they know, because they can feel it, but sometimes women need to hear what men need to say, for both to be able to move on, for good.

Chapter Thirteen

(Intentions)

What could Donovan's intentions have been when they met eighteen years ago. Was he interested in just having fun in a distant relationship with someone that he could sleep with every now and then, or was he searching for love with someone. Gabriela remembers when they first began dating that Donovan genuinely seemed to love her, and he seemed to be happy to have found love with someone, as if maybe he got more from their relationship then he expected. So if what she felt was the case, then what happened to change things?

Maybe if Gabriela had known the answer to that question she could've tried to make it right again. But things would change and she would have no idea what caused the change.

To her, it just doesn't make sense for a man to seek a woman out, ease her into a relationship with the promise of love, give her a sense of security and then snatch it all right from under her feet, and think that she does not need to understand what happened. Maybe men are just dense that way, or maybe some of them just don't care; she doesn't really know.

The hardest part of dealing with Donovan, just like with some other men, is getting them to just come out and say what's true; truth like this, I don't love you anymore, or I don't want to be with you anymore, when they want to move on, or I will never marry you, when they know they never will.

Of course, there's always intuition, and like Gabriela, most women know what they know, because they can feel it, but sometimes women need to hear what men need to say, for both to be able to move on, for good.

By now, Donovan knows that Gabriela is the type of woman who needs to hear the obvious, which is probably why he won't say it. He knows that saying to her what is true, may just give her the strength she needs to move on. If he tells her that she's not the woman that he hopes to one day end up with, then maybe that might give her the strength she needs to let him go; if he says he does not love her anymore, she will move on. Maybe hearing the obvious from his own mouth, that he will never marry her, will give her the strength to move on, and not go back; maybe.

She and Donovan are at a place where they both want to be happy; the problem is that they both need different things to be happy; they need to do different things and they need to be different people in order to be happy together.

For Gabriela, her life has always been pretty simple when it came to Donovan. She has always been happy being with just him; nothing really complicated for her. She's attempted to go out with other men, but really, she decided long ago that he was the person that she wanted to live her life alongside. If it were up to her Donovan is the man that she would spend her life with; no doubt about it.

Donovan on the other hand, talks a lot about being happy as well. He reminds Gabriela all the time that life is short and he just wants to be happy. Happiness, for him, seems to be, being able to do as he pleases, which would include coming and going as he pleases and maybe while in the midst of his comings and goings he may meet Ms. Right.

Because he'd been married before, maybe he knew that marriage does not always allow someone to do the things that they feel would make them happy, in the way that they view happiness. Sometimes marriage expects a lot from people and selfishness won't allow for some people to have a successful marriage.

On occasion Donovan tells her that she views their present relationship based on things that happened in the past with other relationships. He tells her that many women tend to make that mistake in relationships. Yet, he doesn't seem to understand that one unsuccessful marriage would not necessarily determine how successful another marriage would be; nor can it determine how happy a person would be in that marriage.

On the other hand, if after eighteen years of a friendship and an on and off relationship with Gabriela, if Donovan knows that she is just not someone that he will ever marry, then she should know that too.

For Gabriela, it's just that simple.

Her Saturdays were lonely, and even when she found a way to fill them, it was not the same as spending time with him. Why he never understood that or never cared, she did not know.

Chapter Fourteen

(Summer Days)

Summer days; there's something about waking up in the morning with the sun shining bright; it puts a different outlook on things. It's as if the sun is telling you to get up and get going; there are places to go and things to do.

Summer is also the time when, like animals, people come out of hibernation. You know how animals hibernate in the winter and then when summer approaches, they shed their old skin and come back to life. Well it's the same with people. They shed their heavy winter clothes and show as much skin as they can get away with showing. It is also the time when women have the hardest time keeping up with their men. It is the time when men would rather not be attached to any one woman; a time when men allow themselves to become more distracted then any one person should be. Some men can't help themselves from becoming distracted and others look for distractions.

If she had to choose, summer would be Gabriela's favorite time of the year, but always finding herself alone has left her with many summer days with no fond memories.

It's summer, and it's Saturday, again, and she knows pretty much what the day will bring. The sun is shining, and as usual she finds herself lying on the bed and looking out the window, wishing she had Donovan to spend the day with. As usual, that would not be the case. She never needed to do anything major. She would have been happy just to do little things like go down the shore for the day, go to dinner and a movie, or just take a long drive just to get away for awhile. Her Saturdays were lonely, and even when she found a way to fill them, it was not the same as spending time with him. Why he never understood that or never cared, she did not know.

Another summer was approaching and Donovan would make the mistake of telling her about his weekend away with family members, while before, all the time, telling her how he worked so hard that he had little time to do anything. Even when he could hear the annoyance in her voice, what he said was "I'm just living life". Maybe his telling her was no mistake after all. If it wasn't, if what happened after, is what he thought would happen, then it worked to his advantage.

Once again, Gabriela would be angry, and would tell Donovan that she didn't want to see him again. At the time she didn't realize how convenient that would be for him. She knew that she would not try herself to reach him again, and as it turned out, they went the entire summer, and a little longer, without seeing or speaking with one another. It was not until summer was over that she received a text message from him telling her how much he'd missed her. Summer was over, so maybe he was tired of doing what kept him busy for the summer. As much as she did not want to see him or hear from him, she was always happy when she did finally hear from him.

He would have her to believe that he worked so hard that he did not have time to do the things that she accused him of doing, and as he always did, he made sure not to give her too much time to get use to moving on without him. Strangely enough, about a month before she would hear from Donovan, Gabriela met someone, whom she thought had interest in her. By then she had convinced herself that she'd had enough of she and Donovan's relationship and that she was ready to allow herself to feel something, for someone else; for someone who made her feel like she was worth spending time with. The time that she spent with him was brief, but she was reminded how good it felt to actually go out on a regular date and have some laughs and a good time with a man. As it turned out, it was no more than a couple of weeks after she spent time with that other man that she heard from Donovan. Once she responded to Donovan's message to her, she found herself back again, in a relationship with him. That's where she stayed.

She asked him once, if he would be coming by for the evening. His response was, "I don't know, I have to play it by ear." She thought to herself, wow, play it by ear; what a thing to say; but she needed to remain calm.

Chapter Fifteen

(Playing It by Ear)

Gabriela learned a long time ago, that the key to having and keeping a smooth, enjoyable relationship with Donovan was not to make too many waves; too many waves like asking questions and forcing him to give some type of answer. Not making waves and not asking questions though, was not always easy for her to do, so she hasn't always managed to keep things running smoothly because that would mean that she would be wise to keep her feelings to herself and that she could not always do.

Donovan thinks that he's good at convincing her that she brings negativity to the relationship when she asks questions. You see, Donovan has always been content with having a relationship with her, on his terms. Although he would always suggest it's her terms, Gabriela knows better.

Again and again, Gabriela finds herself accepting mediocrity in a relationship that keeps her feeling happy and sad at the same time. Sometimes happy because, like now, she and Donovan have been spending much more time together, regularly, and sometimes sad because the time they've spent together has still not taken them outside of her home.

As mysterious as he's always been in everything that he does, he mysteriously started spending time with Gabriela regularly and seeming as if it were something that he wanted to do. Now Gabriela knows to go along with the flow, because even though she has no idea where this willingness to semi-commit is coming from, she does understand that questioning Donovan about it, slowly but surely would drive him away.

He has a problem with any deep, serious and genuine conversation that would pit him in a corner to answer questions that he doesn't like to or want to answer. He would surely distance himself as mysteriously as he starting showing up.

Donovan is fine with showing up as long as he can do it on his terms. Showing up on his terms means coming and going when he pleases; no questions asked. Any questions about when he may be coming or how long he may be staying, once he gets there, should be left unasked by Gabriela, because that would be expecting too much from him. She asked him once, if he would be coming by for the evening. His response was, "I don't know, I have to play it by ear." She thought to herself, wow, play it by ear; what a thing to say; but she needed to remain calm.

Gabriela felt that she had been pretty accommodating, so why not ask what he meant by that. In pure Donovan form he responded to her question saying "I didn't know if I would feel like going home tonight," leaving her thinking again, why does she do this to herself?

Although Donovan always seemed to have the upper hand, and even though she's happy, for now, it's not like Gabriela to remain silent when bothered by something. So she finds herself having to decide whether to enjoy the ride, for however long it will last, or to possibly bring the good time they are having together, to an end.

Right now she feels, again, the way she use to feel when they were first together; waking up with him in his apartment as he got up for work. Then he'd leave the house and always kiss her goodbye. Then it felt like nothing could get any better than that. She enjoyed being in love. So to have even a little of that feeling back now, meant a lot to her, no matter how short a time it may last.

She has been traveling on this road to some sense of happiness with Donovan for such a long time; she just wants to get him on the same road with her. Rather, she has been riding on the same rollercoaster for years. Maturity has helped her to understand him and to accept his ways a little easier, but it has certainly not changed how long the ride.

Even in her darkest times she still believes that he loves her. She convinces herself, no matter what is happening, that he couldn't possibly be a part of this relationship, for all these years, and not love her. No one could; could they?

Chapter Sixteen

(He Loves Me, He Loves Me Not)

Gabriela has always been torn by one question; does Donovan really love her, or not? She wants desperately to believe that he does, or else why would he have stayed around this long. You know like the pedals from the rose, he loves me, he loves me not. She is reminded of just that when she thinks of their relationship.

Sometimes, even in her darkest times she still believes that he loves her. She convinces herself, no matter what is happening, that he couldn't possibly be a part of this relationship for all these years and not love her; no one could; could they? She knows that, like him, she has her faults. He has accepted them and over the years he's continued the relationship in spite of them, so he must still love her.

There are times when she feels as if he does not love her at all; times when he has said or done something, maybe not to hurt her intentionally, but that did hurt her. How could he not know? There are times when he does nothing at all.

Recently he did something that he had not done in a very long time. Donovan gave her flowers. She was very happy about that. For so long she'd wondered after nearly twenty years, how could he not know how much giving her or sending her flowers meant to her. Again, she could only assume that he is either clueless or that he just didn't care. Gabriela even knows that no man, after so many years is going to treat you the same way they treated you when you first met; you know, as if you were special; why would they need to; why would they have to? It's too much work for them when they first have to do it, but most men feel it necessary. So why would they continue to do something, causing them extra work and money, when they feel it's no longer necessary?

When holidays come around the games always begin. It's pretty much just like what summer brings, it's just here and there. Usually Gabriela can't reach him at all. She's usually unable to talk to him until he decides to reach her. By that time he has done all he's needed to do; the day has gone by and he has his excuses or his reasons why she was unable to reach him. According to Donovan, he had to work, leaving them no time to do anything together, or he never received her call on his phone. Sometimes the reception is bad depending on where he is, or so he says.

Cell phones; oh my god! The use of cell phones has made cheating and deceit an all around art form. When Gabriela is talking to Donovan on his cell phone, for all she knows he could be around the corner or in the next state. She tries not to think about the so many other places he could be.

Maybe he does genuinely love her. Maybe he has done the best that he knows how, to show his love for her, although she thinks that he can do better. Some men have no idea how to show the woman that they love that they love them. They think that it's enough just to come by.

After so many years have gone by so has that special love or any extra special treatment, because even though someone may love you, you have become just like a job that they show up to because they are expected to.

Clearly Donovan's idea of loving her is different from her idea of loving him. She is reminded sometimes of the book "Men Are From Mars, Women Are From Venus", because there are times when a week goes by, and when she finally speaks to Donovan, she's a little annoyed because for her a whole week has gone by with them not having any contact with one another, but Donovan would ask her why is she so upset, it's only been a week. That's just typical of the entire relationship. For a woman, dealing with that kind of logic is just hopeless. She wonders, why not marriage? They both have been dealing with the "for better, or for worse" for quite some time.

Even in the disagreements and their distancing themselves from one another for long periods of time, there is one non-committing thing that Donovan has always told Gabriela and that he has remained true to. He has always told her that he would make love to her forever; not that he would love her forever. For that, she is always able to find him. Like many men, for that, he pretty much shows up when he wants to and sometimes when he feels that it would be in his best interest to do so.

After all this time, Gabriela doesn't even know what to call Donovan. Who is he to her? Is he her man? Is he her lover, or her friend? If a time comes where she has to introduce him to friends, who should she say he is, especially with all the history they've had together? Is it fair for her to have to introduce him as just a friend? Is it fair for her to be introduced as his friend?

Now that they have been together for so long she has given up on labeling their relationship as dating. After all, dating is what you do when you first meet and you spend an appropriate amount of time trying to get to know one another.

Maybe Donovan doesn't realize this, but after nearly two decades together, two people are no longer dating, and if they've yet to marry, and that decision is not a mutual one, then there's something wrong. After a certain amount of time you either want to marry or you move on. At least Gabriela knows, that's the way it should be, so why has it not been that way for her and Donovan.

Clearly she and Donovan has had a long lasting friendship, but is it fair to her to just introduce him as her friend, especially since he gets privileges far beyond what a friend would get. He even gets the same privileges that a husband would get.

When Gabriela is approached by other men and asked if she's married, she has the easy answer to that. When she's asked, do you have a man? after all these years, that's not so easy for her to answer. She's even unsure about whether she's seeing someone or not. In their relationship she's not sure if seeing someone means that she's unavailable. She's afraid to even hear how he would introduce her now, to his family and his friends. How did she fall victim for so long, to emotions that would allow her to be in this position?

Gabriela has learned over the years how to live with being alone, because in their relationship, when things go bad, she finds herself with plenty of alone time. She wonders sometimes what his answer would be if he were asked if he was seeing someone. She's afraid that if he were approached and asked if he were in a relationship with anyone that his response would surely be, no.

She knows how foolish it is, being in a relationship with a man, and still asking herself, who is she to him and who does he want to be to her. She's tried very hard to make the best of a relationship that has made her to look and feel foolish and desperate.

She has always thought of herself as a romantic, so love and relationships have always been important to her. It is one of the reasons why she's so committed when she falls in love; why she's allowed herself to remain in a relationship with a man who doesn't seem to either, understand, know or care about what makes her happy.

Donovan is at the top of his game right about now. He must feel really good about himself right now. Let's see; for years, he's been able to maintain a friendship with sexual privileges with the same woman and he's managed to do so without any obligations of marriage. He's even learned how to quickly thwart the topic of marriage and he only seems to show some commitment to the relationship when it's on his terms.

Who should she say he is to her? Well, like with most things, when it comes to the two of them, she doesn't have the answer. So for now, she guesses that he'll just remain her friend, Donovan.

She cannot recall a time when she's ever committed to, or worked so hard for any relationship.

Chapter Seventeen

(One Foot in-One Foot Out)

At night, when Gabriela lays beside Donovan, she feels safe. When they're able to joke with one another, she feels happy. When they share stories of how their day went, she feels included. To her, everything feels good, yet Donovan still has one foot in and one foot out of the relationship. How does she deal with a man who is half in, and half out of the relationship? How does she begin to gauge the reason for it? What fear is he carrying that he won't put his whole self into them; into building a life together?

Gabriela has always felt as if she were being tested by Donovan. It seems as though he waits for her to make a mistake. He relies on her to say the wrong thing or do the wrong thing so that he will have an excuse to distance himself further from any commitment, and so to justify why things just aren't working the way they should.

For them it always seemed to be the wrong time. In the eighteen years that they've known one another, the right time has always turned out to be the wrong time. She cannot recall a time when she's ever committed to, or worked so hard for any relationship to work out. He would never know this, but she's put a lot of work into trying to be the person that she thinks that he would be happier being with. After all, she's been trying to make their relationship work for very close to half her life. If she had put as much time, effort and heart in other areas of her life as she has done with her relationship with Donovan over the years, surely she would have been successful at something that she could be proud of, by now.

Donovan's expectations of their relationship are not quite realistic, which is surprising to Gabriela. For a man of years and maturity you would think that he would know that no relationship is always perfect, calm, peaceful and without problems. It is just not realistic for any man or woman to expect that from a relationship, whether it's a friendship, a romance or a marriage. When the inevitable argument or the many disagreements come, that does not mean that the love goes out of the relationship. She's always thought that that is when the love and the friendship and the romance were being tested the most.

The funny thing is, that in his mind, after all the years they've shared, he really tries to leave himself room for an out, while at the same time making sure that she's locked in. He would tell her that if she decided to leave him for another it would not be fair of him to get in the way of her happiness and that he believes that she would not find any one better for her than him.

Gabriela knows that he would question the love that she claims to have for him if she left him for someone else, even when he's not completely committed to their relationship. Keeping her on lock down in the relationship, gives him the comfort of knowing that she's his whenever he wants her to be. Having some other man touch her would definitely not sit well with him. He's always been willing to accept her heart and her love completely without giving the same, one hundred percent.

One of the reasons why Donovan will not bring himself to marry Gabriela is because he already has a family; a family that she's not a part of. It's that family, even though he has love for her that still pulls the strings to his heart. It's the family that he wants to spend time with during holidays or on special occasions. He wants to have Gabriela as one part of his life, but being with her cannot interrupt the other part of his life; which brings us back to his terms. Donovan knows that marriage to her would change things. Marriage to her would automatically make her his family.

When you have one foot in a relationship and one foot out you're already setting the relationship up for failure, which is what Donovan has always done. He's constantly looking for something to go wrong, depriving the both of them of the chance of having a caring and loving relationship.

Like many couples, Gabriela and Donovan have had their differences, but even with those differences there has to be more to their relationship than just the convenience of being together. Is it their differences that makes him fear making another mistake; marrying again?

Whoever it is that he is waiting for her to become, she will probably never become. She's worked so hard trying to improve the person she is, not just for him, but for herself, but the expectation of her becoming that perfect person; the person who never speaks her mind, the person who's afraid to communicate when communication is necessary, the person who doesn't make decisions for herself, will probably never happen. He knows her. No man knows her better. She has to be accepted and loved for who she is. She really doesn't know how to be anyone else.

Over the years she has learned that there are things that she needs to change about herself, but no one should expect her to change who she is, not even Donovan.

She'd missed out on all the big dances; the dances that every girl dreams about being a part of. Those times in her life she will never be able to go back to again.

Chapter Eighteen

(The Big Dance)

How could Gabriela have been so unfortunate as to miss out on every big dance? The biggest dance, of course, is that special day; the day that many women hope and prepare for most of their life. It's not likely that she will get to the big dance now. She'd always seen herself being there one day, but it hasn't happened and even if she were asked it wouldn't be as she had always hoped it would be; not now. Time would have changed all that. She would not have the opportunity for her father to walk her down the aisle nor would they have the opportunity for the father-daughter dance.

She'd imagine to herself, many times, going to bridal shops and trying on beautiful wedding gowns, imagining how she would look had she been fortunate enough for that special day to come. She figured why not; she could easily spend a day trying on a number of dresses: after all, only she would know that she really wasn't a bride to be. Maybe one day she could do it anyway.

She would not get the opportunity to celebrate her happiness with the man that she loves and all their family and friends, on that most special day. To add even more salt to the wound, every once in a while she finds herself being invited to share in someone else's nuptials. She's attended so many weddings of young people, reminding her of what she'd missed out on. Each wedding she attends, she promises herself that that will be the last one, but she finds herself attending another and another one after that. Young or older, they are her friends and it would be unfair to take her feelings of missing out, out on them. Every time she attends one of her friend's wedding she has to work really hard to keep herself out of a dark place, where she wishes it were her.

Ironically, her wedding is not the only big dance that she's missed out on. Gabriela never attended her prom. She remembers her senior year in high school and dating and being in love with a man who was four years her senior. He didn't have much interest in attending the prom. He was not the kind of man who would be interested in attending a senior prom. Unbeknownst to him though, that was alright with her, because as foolish as this may sound to her now, he was shorter in stature than she was, and even though she loved him, she did not want to go to the prom with him either. He never knew that and he probably was relieved not to have to be a part of it.

Gabriela has always regretted not attending the prom. She should not have let such a silly thing keep her from attending her own prom. It's a special celebration that students should try to be a part of if they can and if he didn't want to go, she should have attended the prom with someone else. It's a time to dress to impress, to feel good about how you look together, and to share the last happy time with your classmates, many of whom you will never see again. It's one of the very first times that women get to wear their first of beautiful gowns.

Having a sweet sixteen party, is another big dance that Gabriela would miss out on as a teenager. Back then, Gabriela, nor anyone she'd known, had ever had a sweet sixteen party. There were probably young ladies having sweet sixteen parties then, but it would not be any of her friends or anyone in her neighborhood that she'd ever heard about. Families in her neighborhood were not able to have fancy sweet sixteen parties, with fancy gowns, in large, cost per plate halls; not the kind of parties that the young girls have today.

She is no different than any other woman who was raised to be all about tradition. During the time when she came up, women were pretty much raised to meet a good man and to one day get married. That is not to say that we were not expected to get a good education and to be able to do for ourselves, but it would be especially nice to be married and to have a family as well.

Yes, she'd missed out on all the big dances; the dances that every girl dreams about being a part of. She will never be able to go back to those times in her life. She'd missed out on special stories to tell her children.

Donovan tells her that watching too much television keeps her living in a fantasy world and maybe that's true to a point, but it reminds her that there are people out in the world who are not just alive, but they are living. It reminds her that there are men out in the world who eventually marry the women that they claim to love and that the fantasy can be real.

This one thing Gabriela can say about herself; she has been in love with love for as long as she can remember.

Chapter Nineteen

(In This Place)

This one thing Gabriela can say about herself; she has been in love with love for as long as she can remember. It is so much of why she believes in relationships; why she convinces herself that they can work, against all odds.

She's confused and drained from being in this place, still; that place where, in her heart, she loves this man and she can't imagine her life without him in it, but she can't get him to want the life with her that she wants with him. What else can she do for him to love her enough to let go of the idea that he doesn't want to commit. She knows that she shouldn't stay but she can't leave either. How does she get out of this place?

When she looks back at past relationships she realizes that she could never have made a life with any of them, but in her heart she knows that she and Donovan could have been happy together and she will always regret that he never gave their relationship, their life, really together, a chance.

It makes sense that now her need to know where their relationship is going has magnified. Many years have passed her by and yet, at times, she still feels alone, even when he's around. She feels herself getting older by the day and as she gets older the need to know where their relationship is going to end up, gets stronger. Maybe to Donovan her insistent pushing to find out where their relationship is going, is a sign of desperation, but to her it would be even more foolish not to want to know and not to ask.

Again, she finds herself lying next to Donovan making an attempt to discuss the future of their relationship, but, as is always the case, he doesn't hear her. It would only take a matter of minutes before he turns himself off from what she is saying, because he knows that the things that she need to be happy in their relationship, he would not be giving her. Whenever their relationship is at a place where they need to talk, he doesn't allow himself to hear her. He does whatever it takes to break away from any conversation that has to do with them.

Sometimes she lies in bed next to him, fighting with herself, thinking about how she can leave a relationship that he doesn't care enough about. It's scary to know that, after all these years, if she leaves, that he would not blink an eye; he would just move on. That would confirm something for her that she doesn't want to know, and that is that she has wasted all these years loving a man who could care less whether she stays or whether she goes. She just couldn't bare the thought of knowing that plain and obvious truth.

Gabriela cannot be happy with Donovan because he's not happy with her. As much as she loves him, the weight of their relationship is sometimes too heavy for her. It feels like a heavy weight that's holding her down and keeping her from doing the things that would make her happy. She knows that she only has herself to blame for not moving on, but that's the place that's she's in.

Gabriela wants to enjoy her life, with him or without him. She wants to travel, big time, to Paris and Hawaii; places that she's never been before. She wants to visit these places with him, but she knows it will never happen.

If she leaves him to move on with her life, she will feel like a special part of her is missing. If she stays in this uncommitted relationship with him then she will never give herself the opportunity to do the things that she wants to do. Donovan won't let himself share her life. She could probably find someone else who would like to spend time with her doing the things that she'd like to do, but even though Donovan doesn't have the time or the desire to spend time with her, he will somehow make her feel as if all her expressions of love to him, meant absolutely nothing. He will not see his part in any of it. He will quietly walk away from their relationship leaving her to feel as if she'd done something wrong to him.

So how can Gabriela get out of this place? Talking to him doesn't really get too far. The answer really is simple to someone who is not in her place, but to her, it's not so simple. There is nothing simple about separating your life from the life of a man that you have loved for so many years. It's nothing simple about it at all.

She's always envisioned what their relationship would be like had it gone from a special friendship to an equally special relationship. If he could just love her, see her, and hear her, the way that she does him, their relationship would be what she'd always envisioned.

For a while something changed and he became the man that she fell in love with years ago

Chapter Twenty

(Last Chance)

In the past year Gabriela and Donovan have been spending time together again. To Gabriela, it feels like they are starting all over again. It feels as if they have met for the very first time and she's seeing the man that she once knew many years ago. It feels so new because they're learning about one another all over again. So many years have gotten between them that Gabriela is learning new things about what he likes to do and what he likes to eat, and what he enjoys talking about, that she didn't know before. Once his heart left her he would never stay put long enough for her to know much at all about him. She doesn't really know what has changed for him, but he seems more at ease with their spending time together.

For a while something changed and he became the man again, that she fell in love with years ago. She feels closer to him and happier with him then she has been in a very long time. The loneliness that she's felt for so long has left her for awhile and Donovan has made her feel special again. The feelings that she had in the past, focusing on what he was doing away from her or who he may have been with, have left her. He could be spending time with someone else; who knows, but Gabriela is no longer consumed by the thoughts of those things that she does not know, or willing to find out. If he is seeing someone it will one day play itself out. The years and maturity, thank God for it, has help her to accept that and to go on with her life with him or without him.

No, they are still not married, but to her it feels as if they are, even if Donovan feels more comfortable and safe seeing it another way.

Gabriela is reminded of the times when he would cook for her. He's cooking for her again simply because it makes her happy and she can see that he's happy to do it for her. It makes her happy the way he quickly puts together breakfast for her before she goes to work. It makes her happy when she comes home from work and he's unexpectedly in the kitchen preparing dinner.

She feels as if his heart is close to hers again. It's not just that Gabriela sees the man that she once knew, but he's made her feel as if he's with the woman that he fell in love with years ago. Her heart feels good when he compliments her about things that she thought she had lost a long time ago or when he gives her that look that a man gives a woman when he likes what he's looking at. Even at her age, she still finds herself toting her phone around the house with her, just so she will not miss his call.

He still works very hard and he's understandably exhausted by the time she gets to see him. It takes a lot of time from their relationship and the time that they are able to spend together, so she tries to make the best of whatever time they have together.

One evening when he didn't work and they were able to spend time together, they did one of the most unlikely things. When Donovan entered the room, Gabriela was listening to old songs on her laptop. Before she realized it, they were enjoying music from both their laptops. She didn't know if that's what couples did when they're nearing fifty or are already there, but it's what they did that evening and she enjoyed it.

Music has a way of bringing people together, especially music that reminds you of your adolescence. They started out listening to music and that led to conversation about both their childhoods. It felt good to talk.

The truth is that she tries to make the best of every moment and every day they spend together, because she knows that one day he will retreat from their relationship again. She carries the fear of what may be temporary between them, again.

Gabriela knows that she is taking a big risk of being heartbroken again, if he decides to leave or if he goes back to the way that things were before, but she's decided that she's willing to take the risk one last time.

Maybe now that they are older and a little wiser and more accepting of one another, things will work out for them this time. Maybe they will grow old together, maybe not.

Maybe this will be their time. If not this time, then there will never be a time for them and hopefully she will move on and accept the friendship that they have always been blessed to have in one another.

She'll never be able to explain why whenever they broke up she'd allow him back into her life. It's a bad place to be because maybe one day he will decide to leave again, but she's decided that she is better with him then she is without him. Too much time has passed.

Without having to say anything, could the years have made their friendship as important to him as it is to her?

Chapter Twenty One

(The Friendship)

Gabriela realizes that she and Donovan may never have the relationship that she wants. Maybe the time will never be right for them. She knows, though, that if they never have the life together that she's always hoped for, that they will always have their friendship.

She's tried, almost too hard, to make their relationship into what she wanted it to be, not accepting that it may not only be the resistance from Donovan, but that maybe God has another plan for the both of them. She still does not know what God's plan may be for them or what will become of them, but she is thankful every day for the friendship and she's always believed that God puts people in one another's lives for a reason.

One day way back when, she met a man, Donovan. She thought maybe he would be the one. Again, as she had done before, she allowed herself to be led into what she thought was a relationship that he wanted with her just as she wanted with him. When she realized that his feelings changed from what she thought they were it was too late for her to turn back and step away; at least that's how she felt the very moment that she realized that something had changed for him.

If only she had not allowed their relationship to turn into something physical; they would have a loving and caring friendship with no strings and no baggage attached.

Had their relationship gone in that direction, maybe then Donovan would have wanted to marry her. After all, sometimes that's just how it goes. Once he realized what her intentions were for them, and probably the intentions of others close to her as well, it sent him running in a totally different direction.

As friends, she's able to go to him about anything to feel better. She's able to do that now, as long as it's not about their relationship. But as always, being in a physical relationship changes things. Every little thing becomes more serious. Every incident between them is magnified, at least by her, because now she's into the relationship deeper than he could ever care to understand. To Gabriela everything warrants concern. Anything that concerns her with the relationship requires some conversation. Everything Donovan says, opens up thoughts of, what exactly does he mean by that. Everything becomes magnified.

To Donovan, however, every potentially big issue is not big at all. It has very little meaning. Sometimes he's not even aware that she has a concern or that there is an issue.

Gabriela sometimes wonders what their friendship means to him. Without having to say anything, could the years have made their friendship as important to him as it is to her? At times, she thinks so and maybe a genuine friendship is all that he's able to give of himself to her.

She always feels at a disadvantage with him, because when it comes to their relationship it's as if he knows something that she doesn't: things that he's never willing to share with her.

She remembers having a conversation with Donovan and telling him that she loves him, but that she can never seem to figure him out. She has always found it difficult to understand him. Donovan responded to her by asking why does she spend time trying to figure him out; why can't she just understand that he is who he is and let it just be that way. Gabriela went on to explain to him that sometimes she needs to figure out what's going on in his head because there's been so many times that she could not seem to understand why he does the things that he does, or the things that he doesn't do. It would make things so much easier for her to deal with or to accept if only she understood the reason for them.

Over the years she's been holding on so tight to what could have been; to what she thought should have been that she took away his desire to be comfortable with just enjoying time with her.

Now, Gabriela feels herself getting closer and closer to just putting all she had hoped for aside, and letting their relationship go as far as it was meant to go. The fight to make it into what she wanted it to be has become way too consuming and way too hard. She loves him now and always, and maybe the way that he has shown her over the years that he loves her is the only way that he knows.

In all the years that they have known one another, if she had not spent so much time concentrating on what she did not get out of her relationship with Donovan, she would admit that there have been so many days that his friendship has gotten her through not so easy times.

If after all their years together they never marry and begin a new life together, she will accept the friend(ship) that God has blessed her with and she will always be grateful for it.

Sometimes relationships are just meant to be friendships and no more than that.

You'll know when you're settling, because you don't feel loved when you settle. You'll know because it's hard to be happy when you settle. You'll know because it's hard to be yourself when you settle.

*****

Last Chapter

(Starting All Over Again)

Donovan was so hard to love. It really didn't matter what Gabriela did to show how much she loved him. A life with her, together as a family, was just not what he wanted. So in the end, they would never have anything more than a friendship. For that friendship, she was happy.

Gabriela has no one to blame but herself for giving her heart, her body and her mind for so many years, to a man, who though he may love her, could not bring himself to want the life with her that she wanted with him. That was her choice. Her love for him is as strong a love as she will ever have for any man, but she understands more now, that what he needs to be happy is just not the same as what she needs to be happy. She believes that he understands what makes her happy, but he will never be able to provide her with it if it means changing who he is to make that happen. Sometimes it's just like that in relationships.

Gabriela was once told by a friend, who happens to be male, that when a woman is in a relationship with a man and she's unhappy, the reason for her unhappiness doesn't matter. Badgering a man to find out if he's cheating won't really get her the answers she wants. Convincing herself that maybe it's something wrong with her or maybe it's something that she did wrong, won't help either. All that matters is that for some reason the relationship is making her unhappy and if she allows herself to settle, she'll never really find happiness with him.

She once heard someone ask the question, what is the difference between compromising and settling? When she heard the question she immediately thought of her relationship with Donovan. She knew then that there was a difference between compromise and settling and she realized which one she had been doing all these years. She knew that compromise had not been making her unhappy in the relationship; it was settling that made her unhappy.

A lot of men say that one of the problems that women have is that they're always trying to change men. What men do not understand, is that woman are not interested in changing them. Changing a man is not their ultimate goal for a successful relationship, and it's not really that important. They don't want to change the person that they came to love.

Women just want men to understand that being willing to compromise, sometimes, in a relationship, in order for the person that you love to be happy, is important. Relationships need compromise from both parties to work. If one person is always doing the compromising in the relationship, there will always be feelings of unhappiness for that person.

You'll know when you're settling, because you don't feel loved when you settle. You'll know because it's hard to be happy when you settle. You'll know because it's hard to be yourself when you settle.

Maybe someday none of this will matter to Gabriela any more than it seemed to matter to Donovan. Hopefully, though, Gabriela's relationship with Donovan will be a guide to other young women who find themselves in the same situation, the same type of relationship to just move on when love stands still, before they convince themselves that they've spent to much time in the relationship to leave now.

Love is strong enough to keep any relationship going for a very long time, but some endings are inevitable.

www.ingramcontent.com/pod-product-compliance
Ingram Content Group UK Ltd.
Pitfield, Milton Keynes, MK11 3LW, UK
UKHW040559210726
13854UKWH00008B/1588

9 781456 731397